The Magic Within

OrangeBooks Publication

1st Floor, Rajhans Arcade, Mall Road, Kohka, Bhilai, Chhattisgarh 490020

Website: **www.orangebooks.in**

© Copyright, 2025, Author

All rights reserved. No part of this book may be reproduced, stored in a retrieval system, or transmitted, in any form by any means, electronic, mechanical, magnetic, optical, chemical, manual, photocopying, recording or otherwise, without the prior written consent of its writer.

First Edition, 2025

ISBN: 978-93-6554-195-3

Discovering Self-Mastery For Kids

THE MAGIC WITHIN

Aahana Gupta

OrangeBooks Publication
www.orangebooks.in

ROADMAP

Preface	2
Step 1: Understanding Yourself	5
Step 2: Time Management	14
Step 3: Organization Skills	26
Step 4: Emotional Management	36
Step 5: Healthy Habits	48
Step 6: Developing Responsibility	57
Step 7: Decision Making and Problem Solving	61
Step 8: Staying Motivated	72
Step 9: Review and Reflection	81

Imagine having a toolkit that helps you stay organized, handle your judgments, and make smart choices. That's self-management!

It's about mastering skills that help you to take efficient and balanced control of your life and reach your goals, no matter how challenging they may be.

Ready to discover how self-management can make your everyday life easier, a lot more productive, and a lot more fun?

But why is self-management important? As the word itself says, you will learn how to manage yourself. Once you learn how to manage yourself, you will notice a change in yourself after using the tips and tricks that are given. Your academic grades will improve, you will grow as a person, and achieving your goals will become a lot simpler. While not having a single bit of stress, you will be able to do all of this so easily, that you will become a master of doing and achieving things.

In this book, I will be teaching you 9 steps that will help you grow and manage yourself in the most perfect way possible.

Before starting the book, rate yourself on these categories:

Category	Rating (out of 10)
Time Management and Prioritization	
Organizational Skills	
Goal Setting and Achievement	
Self-Discipline and Focus	
Stress Management Techniques	
Problem-Solving Abilities	
Adaptability to Change	
Responsibility for Actions	
Decision-Making Skills	
Reflective Practice and Improvement	

Did you know that there was a man who worked a regular job until he was 66 years old? He didn't make enough money to take care of his wife, so he started cooking chicken at home to earn more. His name was Colonel Sanders, and he worked hard to make his chicken delicious. Millions of people now enjoy his tasty chicken every day. And today, his shop is none other than KFC!

So never question yourself about how much you can do because there are so many things out there that await your arrival.

Never judge yourself based on the things that you haven't done. Everything comes from experience. If you haven't experienced something, you can never know if it is for you or not.

Your <u>strengths</u> are the areas that align with your qualities and that you have experience and interest in. Your strengths can be anything you enjoy doing. <u>Weaknesses</u> are the tasks or skills we find challenging. They show us where we can improve while getting better and growing stronger.

To figure out your strengths, you could ask questions like these to yourself:

1. What is something I do when I am bored which makes me happy?
2. When do I feel most proud of myself?
3. What skills and talents do I have that I can be recognized for?

4. Which achievement of mine am I proud of?

5. What comes naturally to me that others might find difficult?

6. In what situations do I feel most confident and capable?

Do you see any common aspects about yourself in the answers? Those are your strengths.

To find out the aspects you don't excel in, or your weaknesses, you could ask yourself:

1. What tasks or activities do I avoid a lot because they are challenging or uncomfortable?

2. When do I feel frustrated or annoyed because of a task?

3. What mistakes do I seem to repeat?

4. What goals have I had difficulty achieving?

5. What skills do I wish I had but find difficult to develop?

6. In what situations do I feel least confident?

7. What tasks do I find boring or draining?

8. When do I feel like I'm not performing at my best?

After identifying your weaknesses, you can use this chart to help turn your weaknesses into strengths.

Weakness	Identifying the issue in detail	What happens if I try to work on it	What will I do to fix it (Time specific)	Was I able to do it

An example of this has been given below:

Weakness	Identifying the issue in detail	What happens if I try to work on it	What will I do to fix it (Time specific)	Was I able to do it
English Spellings	I am unable to spell English words very easily like necessary, exciting, accommodation, etc.	I tried to memorize the spellings, but I kept on forgetting them and repeating the errors	I will list down the words I find difficult to spell and practice writing them and their techniques for at least 15 minutes every day for 1 month	I practiced my spelling every day for one month and I am now able to spell all the words properly

You can fill in the last column after you have completed your deadline.

This way, you will be able to understand your limits and will allow you to push yourself beyond them. You should never be ashamed of having weaknesses because everyone has weaknesses. What matters is what you do to turn them into your strength.

To flourish even more, setting goals is very important. Goals are your winner's ribbon as they would take you to heights you can't even imagine. This is why planning your goals smartly is essential.

So, let's create SMART Goals!

S - Specific

M - Measurable

A - Achievable

R - Relevant

T - Time Bound

How do these work? Look at the example:

GOAL 1	
Specific - *Talk about the details of your goal.*	I want to improve my English spelling by focusing on the words I commonly misspell and expanding my vocabulary from

	my current reading list to an advanced level
<u>Measurable</u> - *State how exactly will you measure this goal*	I will practice spelling 10 new words each week and take a quiz which I make to check my progress every Friday. I'll track my progress by recording my quiz scores and noting any words I consistently misspell.
<u>Achievable</u> - *Talk about how will you achieve this goal*	I will use spelling apps and create flashcards to study these words, dedicating 15 minutes every day to practice. I will also review the words in context by using them in sentences or writing short paragraphs
<u>Relevant</u> - *Mention how is the goal relevant in your life, how is it going to benefit you*	Improving my spelling will help me get better grades in English class and enhance my writing skills. This will also help make my writing clearer and more professional.
<u>Time Bound</u> - *Write how will you time yourself for this goal by giving yourself*	I will achieve a 90% accuracy rate on my weekly quizzes by the end of the next two months. This

deadlines and allotted time.	timeframe gives me enough time to see improvement and adjust.

Goals can be set in a period of a few weeks, as well as a few years. The goals that are set for the near future, like "I want to finish 3 books in the next month" or even "I want to score full marks on my test next week" are known as short-term goals.

Goals that are set over a longer period, are known as Long-term goals. For example, "I want to become a musician and perform at a national level in the next 10 years". Setting both goals is extremely important as they give you direction and motivation in areas where you require.

REWARD SYSTEM

This method will help you achieve your goals better. You can always plan your goals in a way where you get a reward for completing them. For heavier tasks, you can have greater rewards, and for simpler tasks, you can have little or no rewards at all.

For example, if you need to finish a 20-page presentation, you can reward yourself by eating your favorite meal or taking a 2-hour long relaxing shower after the completion of the task. Completing your goal is a reward as you have one less task left to do but when you reward yourself for doing something like this, the reward feels sweeter, and your brain gets motivated to do more and accomplish the goals while keeping a healthy mentality.

Fill in your SMART Goal table below:

GOAL	
Specific - *Talk about the details of your goal.*	
Measurable - *State how exactly will you measure this goal*	
Achievable - *Talk about how will you achieve this goal.*	
Relevant - *Mention how is the goal relevant in your life, and how is it going to benefit you.*	
Time Bound - *Write how you will time yourself for this goal by giving yourself deadlines and specific allotted time.*	

You can have as many goals as you like! Look at the example and use the table below to plan your goals weekly.

Year	2025						
Goal		Getting into a routine					
Incentive		Movie night with friends					
January	Sun	Mon	Tue	Wed	Thu	Fri	Sat
	1	2	3	4	5	6	7
Wake up at 6 AM	○	○	○	○	○	○	○
Meditation	○	○	○	○	○	○	○
Walk in the garden/play a sport	○	○	○	○	○	○	○
Eat food on time	○	○	○	○	○	○	○
Not getting angry	○	○	○	○	○	○	○
Helping with Chores	○	○	○	○	○	○	○
Progress %							
Complete							
incomplete							

Now, fill your table!

Year							
Goal							
Incentive							
	Sun	Mon	Tue	Wed	Thu	Fri	Sat
	○	○	○	○	○	○	○
	○	○	○	○	○	○	○
	○	○	○	○	○	○	○
	○	○	○	○	○	○	○
	○	○	○	○	○	○	○
	○	○	○	○	○	○	○
Progress %							
Complete							
incomplete							

Now that you understand yourself, time for Step 2, which is managing time.

STEP 2
TIME MANAGEMENT

I think the scariest thing out there is time. It doesn't stop for anyone and keeps on moving relentlessly. But this constant flow of never-ending time can benefit us in hefty amounts. Using time effectively is crucial because we have so much to do in very limited time. In this limited time, we need to study, participate in other activities, and still find moments for ourselves—whether it's watching TV, wearing a face mask, or just relaxing. Managing our time well ensures we can balance all these aspects every day to make the most out of all the time we have.

What will happen if you don't manage your time well? You will end up not reaching your deadlines, your quality of work will degrade, have an increased stress, and you will start procrastinating on everything. We can't let that happen, can we?

There are many ways that we can manage our time. First, Let's learn how to make effective schedules!

It's very important to know your limit so you can plan your activities. A good schedule should have detailed tasks with sensible and doable time boundaries.

An example of a good schedule for a weekend is given below:

TIME	ACTIVITY	NOTES
8:00 - 9:00	Wake up & get ready	Get fresh, shower, and eat something healthy to start the day well

9:00 - 10:00	Finish all school homework	Finish homework and do difficult topics if time is left
10:00 - 11:00	Outdoors	Go out and play
11:00 - 1:00	Get Productive	Read a book, sketch, paint, draw
1:00 - 2:00	Break	Eat lunch and enjoy
2:00 - 3:00	Cleaning	Organize room and clean cupboards
3:00 - 4:30	Study time	Self-study - do difficult topics and tasks, take assistance from YouTube, etc.
4:30 - 6:30	Outdoors	Go outside and play
6:30 - 8:00	Get fresh + Dinner	Take a shower and have dinner
8:00 - 8:30	Hobbies	Practice the guitar, piano
8:30 - 9:00	Winding up	Pack school bag and take out uniform for the next day

| 9:00 | Sleep | Put on light music and sleep |

This schedule has achievable time boundaries, is not very heavy, and allows you to cover all your tasks. To make a schedule, you need to do the following:

1. Make a To-Do list of all the things you need to cover with deadlines and specifications
2. Break down larger tasks into bits to make it easier
3. Allocate an estimated time for each task
4. Number the tasks based on priority
5. Start with any comfortable format (list, table, etc.) to make your schedule
6. Start placing the tasks based on priority
7. Give enough time and activities between tasks so you don't burn out and overwhelm yourself
8. Color code your schedule to make it more organized and easier to understand
9. Track your progress - Check or cross out tasks that have been done
10. Stick to your plan

It is not important to plan yourself from minute to minute if you don't have a lot of tasks to complete. You could even make a time allocation chart, in which you only write the things you need to accomplish along with its minimum time boundaries.

For example.

- Read - 45 minutes
- Practice Singing - 45 minutes
- Study - 1.5 hours
- Homework - 1 hour
- Go out and play - 2 hours

This will help you achieve your requirements with minimum effort in creating a schedule.

EXAMPLE: You have 2 long tasks due by midnight and 3 short tasks due tomorrow afternoon, and you have only 3 hours today and 1 hour tomorrow to do so. How will you manage?

Here comes the skill of <u>Prioritizing</u>.

Prioritizing is important because it helps us focus on what's important first. When we decide which task or goal is most important, we can better manage our time and make our work more efficient. This means we won't waste time on less important things and can achieve our more important goals Prioritization can also help reduce stress by clarifying what we need to do and in what order.

But in this case, how do I prioritize?

First, write down all the things you need to do along with their deadlines and the estimated time you will take to complete it:

Task	Due date	Estimated Time
1 long essay	midnight	1.5 hours
1 presentation	midnight	2 hours
2 forms	Tomorrow afternoon	40 mins (20 mins each)
1 100-page book to be read	Tomorrow afternoon	30 mins

In this case, the priority would be on the longer tasks as they are due earlier as well as more time-consuming. So, you would do your essay, then your presentation in the first 3 hours along with one form and would finish your remaining 2 tasks in the 1 hour you have tomorrow.

Let's take one more example:

It's 4 PM on Monday, and you have a tight deadline ahead.

- The History Essay is due by midnight tonight,
- The Math Project must be completed by midnight tomorrow.

- The Science Worksheet is due tomorrow afternoon
- English Reading Assignment is due tomorrow afternoon
- Prepare for a Geography Quiz is due tomorrow afternoon

You need to strategically manage your time to ensure everything gets done.

Let's create the task table:

Task	Due Date	Estimated Time
History essay	midnight	1.5 hours
Math project	Midnight tomorrow	2 hours
Science worksheet	Tomorrow afternoon	30 mins
English Assignment	Tomorrow afternoon	15 mins
Geography quiz	Tomorrow afternoon	15 mins

Current time: <u>4 pm</u>

Your day can be planned as:

4:00 pm - 5:30 → Finish history essay

6:30 pm - 7:30 pm → work on math project

(next day)

9 am – 10 am → Finish all 3 assignments

10:30 am - 11:30 am → Finish math project

This way, you have ensured to complete your work on time. It's best to plan all your work to avoid last-minute stress and trouble which would lead to sacrificing other leisure activities in your daily routine.

This example can also be done more easily, using the ABC method of prioritization.

A: High Priority – These tasks are both urgent and important. They have a significant impact on your goals and need to be done as soon as possible.

B: Medium Priority – These tasks are important but not urgent. They should be done after completing A tasks, as they still contribute to your goals but have fewer immediate deadlines.

C: Low Priority – These tasks are neither urgent nor particularly important. They can be done if time permits or delegated if possible

Categorize Tasks:

- A
    - Finish History Essay (urgent and important)
    - Start Math Project (important and approaching deadline)

- B
    - Complete Science Worksheet (important but not immediate)
    - Prepare for Geography Quiz (important but not immediate)
- C
    - Read for English Assignment (less urgent, less impact)

Make your own schedule by prioritizing tasks:

- List down your tasks:
    - _____
    - _____
    - _____
    - _____
    - _____
    - _____

- Prioritize them using the ABC method:
    - A:
        - _____
        - _____

- B:
  - _____
  - _____
- C:
  - _____
  - _____

- Now, make a schedule to align these tasks accordingly:

Time	Task	Notes

- Remove all distractions from your surroundings while doing the tasks
- Color code the schedule to make it more appealing

Now that you have understood how to organize your time, let's learn how to organize yourself.

Step 3
Organization Skills

Along with managing your time, managing your surroundings and work is also very important.

I remember when I was younger, I would leave everything messed up in my room and would think 'Oh, I'll do it later' and that later never came. It is now that I have realized how important it is to keep things organized. I learned that a clean room makes everything easier and less stressful for me. When my room is clean, I can find things faster and it keeps me at ease.

Step 1 of being organized is having a <u>tidy space</u>. The room where you live, the table where you study, the bathroom that you use, everything needs to be clean and the things should be in their designated spaces because if your everyday surroundings like your room cannot be clean, the space in your mind will also never get cleaned. This is why having a tidy and organized space is very important.

How do you have a clean and organized space though?

- **Creation of routines**
    - Have a daily habit of spending a few minutes each day cleaning up (putting your clothes away, books inside, stationary in one place)
    - Deep clean at least once a month to clean the spaces and reorganize them

- **Decluttering**
    - Have monthly sorting sessions where you go through all your stuff and only keep those that you need. Donate and recycle things that are in good condition but not required by you.

   - Start small. Pick one area or category (e.g., a drawer or books).
   - Sort Items: Categorize into Keep, Donate, and Trash.
   - Make Decisions: Quickly decide what to keep based on use and necessity.
   - Organization: Store kept items neatly, using containers or shelves.
   - Dispose: Donate or throw away unwanted items immediately.

- **Clean-up habits**
    - Clean as You Go: Tidy up while you're doing tasks. For example, clean up after eating or working on a project.
    - One Touch Rule: Avoid moving items around. Put things away in their proper place the first time you handle them.

- **Checklists**
    - o Daily Checklist: Include tasks like making the bed, putting away dishes, and tidying up toys or books.
    - o Weekly Checklist: Include tasks such as vacuuming, washing windows, and cleaning out the refrigerator.

- **Accessible essentials**
    - o Easy Access: Store frequently used items where they are easy to reach.
    - o Avoid Overcrowding: Don't overload shelves or drawers. Leave space to find things easily.

- **Practice Mindfulness**
    - o Be Aware: Pay attention to clutter as it accumulates and address it promptly.
    - o Create a Habit: Make cleaning a regular part of your daily routine to keep your space consistently tidy.

Example: Think of your desk like a tidy backpack. Your notebooks are in one place, your pencils are in a pencil case, and your homework is neatly stacked.

When you need something, you find it right away, just like reaching into a well-packed backpack. Whereas, on the other hand, your desk is like a backpack that's been tossed around. Your notebooks are scattered, pencils are lost among crumpled papers, and you can't find your homework. It's going to be like digging through a messy backpack to find your favorite book. Not very practical, right?

Being organized not only is visually tidy but also makes it easier to locate stuff, leading us to not waste time on activities like finding books, and putting the same time into doing something more productive

To organize your schoolwork,

You can use methods like:

- Having a binder to segregate your notes into subjects while having labels which would make it easier to locate your work

- Creating a color-coded system - Allocating subjects different colors to identify them easily (putting math in an orange folder, biology in a green folder, English in a red folder, etc.)

- Having a list of all your tasks and deadlines so you can plan your time and submissions accordingly

- Having a pencil case and drawer organizers to segregate stationary

- Having digital folders on your computer for the digital files to be aligned and organized based on their subjects

Imagine you have a large binder divided into sections for each subject: Math, Science, English, and History. Each section has its pocket folder to keep worksheets and handouts. You use a color-coded system where Math is blue, Science is green, English is red, and History is yellow. Each subject's section and folder are clearly labeled. You keep your planner updated with homework deadlines and test dates. Your desk is tidy, with only your current homework and study materials on it. Your pencil case is filled with pens, pencils, and a highlighter, and your textbooks are neatly stacked on a shelf.

This setup will help you find what you need quickly and will keep everything in its place, making schoolwork easier to manage, and having one less thing on your conscious! Having a clear space means having a clear mind!

Example:

Morning Routine: Jamie spends five minutes reviewing his daily itinerary. He arranges his homework into priority order, makes sure his backpack is fully loaded with everything he needs for school, and consults his planner to find out when assignments are due. It is easier to start your day with a clear plan of action in your mind!

After-School Routine: After school, Alex spends 10 minutes sorting through his backpack. He immediately keeps important papers into labeled folders, put textbooks back on the shelf, and places his homework on his desk. This way, everything is in its proper place, and it is easier for Alex to focus on homework and prepare for the next day, without an ounce of any discomfort due to disorganization.

End-of-Day Cleanup: Each evening, Jordan spends 10 minutes tidying his study table. He puts away any random school supplies, organizes notes into his proper folders, and clears off the desk. This habit helps Jordan start the next day with a clean and organized space, making it easier to focus on new tasks while also having plenty of time for himself.

Weekly Check-In: Every Sunday, Tina sets aside 30 minutes to review her homework assignments, upcoming tests, and extracurricular activities. She uses this time smartly and updates her daily planner, organizes her school materials, and prepares for the week ahead. This habit helps Tina stay organized and manage her time effectively to reduce last-minute rushes.

ROOM CLEANUP CHALLENGE!!!

You must apply all the advice given in this chapter to complete this challenge and clean your room enjoyably and productively! Organizing your room is what you want to accomplish. Fill the table to make your clean-up effective and fun:

CLEANUP CHALLENGE	
Area to clean (e.g. drawers, cupboard, study table)	
Picture of the area currently:	
In how long I will be able to clean it (Start the timer):	
START CLEANING!!	
How long did it take to clean it:	
Picture of the area after cleaning:	
Did I clean and wipe the surfaces as well?	
How much would you rate yourself based on this cleaning out of 5?	

BACKPACK CLEANING!!

In this activity, we will be cleaning your backpack. You should do this at least once a week to stay organized.

1. Backpack Unpacking Party!

Step 1: Dump everything out of your backpack and lay it out on a table or floor. Pretend you're on a treasure hunt and discover what's hiding in there!

Step 2: Sort your items into categories: Books, Stationery, Personal Items, and Extras. Use colorful bins or boxes to make it look like a sorting game!

2. Clean-Up Dance-Off!

Step 3: Shake out any crumbs from your backpack and wipe it a wipe-down. Turn this into a fun mini-dance party and play your favorite songs to enjoy this process even more.

3. Keep or Toss Challenge!

Step 4: Decide which items are essential and which ones can be left out. Challenge yourself to keep only the things you need. Imagine if you are leaving the empty spaces for new adventures.

4. Compartment Puzzle!

Step 5: Pack your items back into your backpack. Use each compartment like a puzzle piece—books in the main section, pencils in the small pockets. See how easily and neatly you can fit everything!

5. Weight Check Fun!

Step 6: Lift your backpack and check its weight. If it's too heavy, lighten it up by removing anything extra. Make it a challenge to balance your backpack like a tightrope walker!

Use this checklist to not forget anything for school!

Item		Did I keep it inside?
Books:	Textbooks	
	Notebooks	
	Laptop	
Stationery:	Pens	
	Pencils	
	Erasers	
	Ruler	
Personal Items:	Water bottle	
	Lunchbox (if applicable)	
	Sanitary Pads (if applicable)	
	Tissues or hand sanitizer	
Extras:	Homework	
	Library books	
	Planner or calendar	
	To-Do list	
	Laptop Charger	

Step 4
Emotional Management

Time for the 4th step of this journey!

As humans, all of us have emotions and every individual has a different way of expressing these emotions. <u>Our emotions are how we respond to anything that happens.</u> Since emotions affect our thoughts, behaviors, and interactions with each other, they hold high extremely importance in our lives. They help us respond to the world around us and illustrate how things matter to us, making it easier to express ourselves

One misconception that people have is that emotions like 'anger' or 'jealousy' or even 'sadness' are negative emotions, but these emotions help us grow as humans if they are felt at the right intensity.

For example, if you are never jealous of someone else's success, you will never be able to pull yourself to that level. If you never get angry about something, you will never be able to voice yourself, and if you never feel sad, you will never know what real pain is, and never appreciate happiness.

Emotions like these help us to be grateful for everything we have in our lives, including every reason to be happy and grateful. Anything and everything is bad if there is an excess of it, which is why we will learn to understand and control our emotions.

Being aware of yourself is extremely important if you want to manage yourself. Understanding what you are, how you are, what you feel, why you feel that, and how your actions affect the others concerned, all come under one category, self-awareness.

Being self-aware is the skill of being responsible enough to take charge of your actions based on your understanding, which has been derived from a pure and clear mind. Self-awareness requires you to be true to yourself and understand and accept the way you are so you can grow and become the best version of yourself.

One of the main topics that comes under the umbrella of self-awareness is emotional awareness. Emotional awareness means to feel and understand yours, and other people's emotions and feelings. It is the ability to recognize what you feel, why you feel, and how to overcome it.

Emotions heavily influence your behavior. For example, you laugh and smile when you are happy. When you feel anger, you make intrusive decisions. Our emotions play a huge role in our daily lives, and it is very important to feel each emotion at its right amount so that we can grow and flourish as a person, helping us along the way

What is the best way to express your emotions?

You can express and understand your emotions by talking to someone who is close to you and who wants the good of you, like your family. <u>Communicating</u> is highly crucial so you can exchange opinions and perspectives.

You can <u>write</u> or <u>journal it</u>. Writing always helps to gather thoughts and find solutions for any given problem. You can write your problems and brainstorm until you reach a root problem, which you can work on and make the problem okay!

If you are feeling overwhelmed, then you can engage in activities like music, dancing, and other hobbies.

It is very important to accept how you are feeling and take further action to learn lessons from those and move on.

For example:

Raya is feeling very sad about her exam results. She got 60% while she was aiming for 80%. She will feel bad about it for some time but then would realize the importance of feeling sad. Being sad will let her brain know that she does not like her score and her brain will tell her "You will do better next time, I know it" and this would motivate her.

Communication with others is very important while feeling these emotions as everyone would have a different view on the situation which would help a lot in understanding the lesson that life is trying to give.

Here are some healthy vs unhealthy expressions of emotions:

1. **Happiness**

    - Healthy Expression: Sharing your joy with others, smiling, and celebrating achievements together.
        - Example: Telling your friends how excited you are about a recent accomplishment and inviting them to celebrate with you
    - Unhealthy Expression: Keeping your happiness to yourself or showing off excessively.

- o Example: Bragging constantly about your success to make others feel bad or isolating yourself because you're too focused on your happiness.

2. **Sadness**

- Healthy Expression: Talking to someone you trust about what's making you sad or writing about your feelings.
    - o Example: Have a heart-to-heart conversation with a friend or write a journal entry to express your sadness.
- Unhealthy Expression: Bottling up your feelings or withdrawing completely from social interactions.
    - o Example: Ignoring your feelings and avoiding friends or isolating yourself for a long time without seeking support.

3. **Anger**

- Healthy Expression: Expressing your feelings calmly and constructively or using physical activity to release tension.
    - o Example: Discussing what made you angry with the person involved calmly or going for a run to cool down.
- Unhealthy Expression: Yelling, being aggressive, or taking your anger out on others.

- Example: Screaming at someone or smashing objects.

4. **Fear**

- Healthy Expression: Talking about your fears with someone you trust or finding ways to confront and manage the fear.
    - Example: Explaining to a parent why you're afraid of something and working together to address it or using relaxation techniques to calm your fears.
- Unhealthy Expression: Avoiding situations that scare you without addressing the root of the fear, or letting fear control your actions completely.
    - Example: Avoiding all social situations because of social anxiety, or letting fear stop you from trying new things.

5. **Disgust**

- Healthy Expression: Communicating your feelings of disgust respectfully and finding solutions to avoid unpleasant situations.
    - Example: Politely expressing to someone that you find a certain behavior uncomfortable and discussing how to address it.
- Unhealthy Expression: Expressing disgust in a rude or judgmental way or allowing it to interfere with your daily life.

- Example: Criticizing or belittling others for their preferences or refusing to participate in activities because of a dislike.

6. **Excitement**

- Healthy Expression: Sharing your enthusiasm with others and participating actively in the things you're excited about.
    - Example: Telling your friends about an exciting event and involving them in the celebration.
- Unhealthy Expression: Overwhelming others with your excitement or being so absorbed in your excitement that you neglect other responsibilities.
    - Example: Constantly talking about your excitement without considering others' reaction

Stress and anxiety can come from different parts of life. School pressure, like too much homework and upcoming tests can make you feel stressed. Problems with friends or feeling left out can cause anxiety. Struggling to balance schoolwork, activities, and personal time can be overwhelming. Worrying about the future, like what job to choose, adds to anxiety. Trying to be perfect and health concerns, either for yourself or loved ones, can also make you anxious. Big changes, like moving to a new school, can create stress too.

Some ways to manage stress and anxiety:

- Not procrastinating
- Finishing work on time
- Distracting yourself from things that are not in your control and still stress you out
- Going out for a walk
- Listening to music
- Deep breathing and meditation
- Healthy eating
- Time management and goals
- Positive thinking

And this list never ends

All emotions should be felt and considered. Feeling any type of emotion is completely normal and one should not be ashamed to feel any emotion. Mood shifts are also very normal so if you randomly go from extremely excited to sad, it's completely okay because, after all, you are human.

Every person reacts to situations and expresses emotions in different ways. What makes one person happy might not have the same effect on someone else which is why it is very important to be self-aware as well as to understand the take of your words on another individual.

The most important thing about emotions is to never be afraid to ask for help. Reaching out about yourself is just another way to be a happier person, tackling all obstacles in your way.

Dealing with emotions isn't very hard till you know what you must do. Look at the table below to get an idea on how to act when you feel different emotions:

Emotion	How to act on it
Happiness	Celebrate your joy with the people you love and indulge in activities you enjoy!
Sadness	Accept that it's okay to be sad and that it will also get fine in a matter of time. Talk to someone about your feelings and find comforting activities to do
Anger	Pause. Take a deep breath and count to 10 before reacting. Express your anger by calmly communicating and putting forth your point. Do an activity that burns this energy positively
Fear	Identify what is scaring you. Break this fear down and tackle each issue one by one. Talk to your parents about how to overcome fears. Sometimes, different perspectives can help.
Disgust	Avoid the things that make you feel disgusted. If it is something in your surrounding space, clean it up and shift your attention to something you find interesting and that makes you happy!

ACTIVITY 1:

Let's create a stress-busters list:

MY STRESS BUSTERS LIST			
Physical activities	Creative activities	Relaxation activities	Social activities
What exercises or sports do you enjoy? E.g. Playing football	*What hobbies or crafts help you relax? E.g. Painting, music*	*What methods help you calm down and feel at ease? E.g. Watching comfort movies*	*What activities with friends or family make you feel happy and supported? E.g. Meeting my friends*

Write whatever activities help you relax and have fun. Make this list and keep it with you whenever you feel stressed so you can do any activity you like to help when you are stressed.

THE MAGIC WITHIN

ACTIVITY 2:

Emotion cards!

What you need:

- Index cards or sturdy paper
- Markers or pens

Create emotion cards. Write different emotions on separate cards. Include a range of emotions to cover both positive and negative feelings. You can use:

- Happy
- Sad
- Angry
- Anxious
- Excited
- Frustrated
- Confident
- Scared

Create Coping Strategy Cards. Write various coping strategies on separate cards that can help manage each emotion. You can use examples like:

- Take deep breaths and count to ten (for Frustrated)
- Talk to a friend or family member (for Sad)

- o Go for a walk or exercise (for Anxious)
- o Write in a journal (for Angry)
- o Listen to music (for Happy)
- o Practice mindfulness or meditation (for Scared)

Shuffle the 2 decks and match them to each other when you feel the emotion so you can know how to help yourself and cope with it!

Eating good and nutritious food is directly related to your mental health. If your gut is happy, you will be happy, which is why it is very important to have healthy eating habits.

There are 2 main aspects of healthy habits: <u>healthy eating</u> and <u>healthy sleeping</u>.

Starting with healthy eating.

A balanced diet is important because it provides the body with the necessary vitamins and minerals it needs to function throughout the day. It increases energy levels, helps control weight, and strengthens the immune system while keeping us healthy. Rich nutrients are essential for things like strong bones and teeth, good digestion, and healthy skin, hair, and nails. A balanced diet can also boost mental health by lowering the risk of depression and anxiety, and it helps prevent chronic diseases like heart disease and diabetes.

How to maintain healthy eating habits?

You can plan your meals to avoid impulsive eating, and all include the necessary nutrients in them.

As it is said, "<u>While eating, listen to your body</u>". Eat until you are satisfied, not full.

You should have a variety of <u>20 fruits and vegetables</u> in 1 week.

List of different fruits and vegetables:

Fruits: Apples, Bananas, Oranges, Strawberries, Blueberries, Grapes, Kiwi, Pineapple, Mango, Pears, Watermelon,

Peaches, Plums, Cherries, Raspberries, Pomegranates, Grapefruit, Apricots, Tangerines, Avocados

Vegetables: Carrots, Broccoli, Spinach, Bell Peppers, Tomatoes, Cucumbers, Sweet Potatoes, Corn, Green Beans, Zucchini, Cauliflower, Kale, Beetroot, Celery, Brussel Sprouts, Radishes, Butternut Squash, Asparagus, Artichokes, Mushrooms

Remember to have your almonds and walnuts every morning!

Stay hydrated and keep on drinking water. Water will help your body stay clean as well as hydrate your skin and make it glow! But there are times when you should not have water, like during meals. Your stomach is a machine and when you eat food, the machine is put to work. This generates heat. If you put water on a working machine, the machine will break down. Similarly, when water enters your stomach while it is working, it will upset your stomach. So, drink as much water as you want, but not during and after 15 minutes of your meal.

To make your meal benefit you more, enjoy your meals! If you can't enjoy your meal, it won't help you in any way.

Compare your energy after eating something healthy which makes you happy and something unhealthy which makes you happy. Feel the difference in your body as when you eat healthy food it increases your energy and keeps you away from all the diseases. By enjoying healthy food, you will forever be inclined towards a healthy diet, helping you in every aspect of your life.

While having good food, having a good way to burn out calories is also very important. Keeping your body active will help boost your physical strength and your mental space.

Engaging in activities like walking or cycling (extremely basic exercise), sports (intermediate exercise), or even agility drills and competitive sports and competitions (advanced exercise) would help keep your body active.

You don't have to do outdoor activities only to stay active, you can also participate in other fun things like dancing, and not alone, but you can do it with your family and friends. You can play games like Twister or even make up your fun games that allow you to be fit!

In these adolescent years, it is important to be fit and eat well as eating gives us energy to play but another factor that affects our energy and growth is our sleep. Sleep is required by our body so our organs can rest and our mind and be at peace. Sleeping helps our body grow which is why it's so crucial to have a good sleep schedule.

Your sleep can be made more productive in many ways like:

- Read a book or a relaxing activity like a word search right before going to bed
- Don't watch any screens for at least 30 minutes before you go to sleep
- Make your bed cozy and comfortable enough so you feel safe and happy in it

- Don't eat sugary snacks or drink caffeine at least an hour you sleep

- Stick to a routine, sleep, and wake up at fixed times every day

- Make sure to have a minimum of 8-9 hours of sleep every day

> Always remember, never focus on the wake-up time but rather on the sleep time because when you sleep at the right time, you will automatically wake up at the right time!

Time for an **Activity**!!

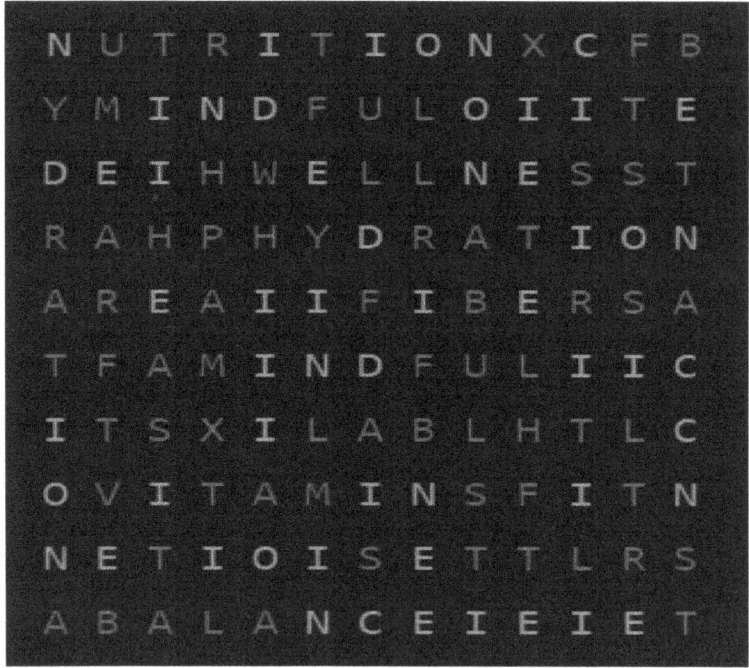

Find these words in the word search:

- ☐ EXERCISE
- ☐ HYDRATION
- ☐ NUTRITION
- ☐ SLEEP
- ☐ WELLNESS
- ☐ MINDFUL
- ☐ FIBER
- ☐ BALANCE
- ☐ FITNESS
- ☐ VITAMINS

Time to be a little more creative and try our hands on some simple and fun-to-make recipes at home!

Recipe number 1: **PEANUT BUTTER BALLS**

Prep Time:	Additional Time:	Total Time:
15 mins	30 mins	45 mins
Servings:	**Yield:**	
12	12 servings	

Ingredients

- ½ cup natural peanut butter, almond butter or sunflower seed butter
- ¾ cup crispy rice cereal
- 1 teaspoon pure maple syrup
- ½ cup dark chocolate chips, melted

Directions

1. Line a baking sheet with parchment or wax paper. Combine peanut butter, cereal, and maple syrup in a medium bowl. Roll the mixture into 12 balls, using about 2 teaspoons for each. Place on the prepared baking sheet. Freeze the balls until firm, about 15 minutes

2. Roll the balls in melted chocolate. Return to the freezer until the chocolate is set, about 15 minutes.

Tips:

To make ahead: Refrigerate in an airtight container for up to 3 weeks.

To melt chocolate, microwave on Medium for 1 minute. Stir, then continue microwaving on Medium, stirring every 20 seconds, until melted. Or place chocolate in the top of a double boiler over hot, but not boiling, water. Stir until melted.

https://www.eatingwell.com/recipe/256999/crispy-peanut-butter-balls/

Recipe number 2: **MANGO FRUIT LEATHER**

Prep Time:	Additional Time:	Total Time:
30 mins	5 hrs	5 hrs 30 mins

Servings:	Yield:
7	7 fruit leathers

Ingredients

- 3 large ripe mangoes, peeled and flesh cut away from the pit
- ½ cup water
- 1 teaspoon lemon juice

Directions

1. Preheat oven to 200°F. Line a large-rimmed baking sheet with a nonstick baking mat.
2. Puree mangoes, water, and lemon juice in a blender until smooth. Pour into a medium saucepan and bring to a simmer over medium heat. Reduce heat to maintain a simmer and cook, partially covered, until reduced to about 2 cups puree, about 20 minutes.
3. Pour the puree onto the prepared baking sheet. With a rubber spatula, very evenly spread into a thin rectangle, no thicker than 1/8 inch thick.
4. Bake until dry to the touch, 4 to 6 hours. Let cool completely.
5. Transfer the fruit leather to a piece of parchment paper (or wax paper) about the same size. Leaving the parchment underneath, roll the fruit leather closed into a long cylinder. Using a sharp knife or scissors, cut into 2-inch-wide strips.

Tips

To make ahead: Store airtight for up to 1 week.

https://www.eatingwell.com/recipe/259995/mango-fruit-leather/

Recipe number 3: **MINI NACHO CUPS**

Prep Time:	Additional Time:	Total Time:
5 mins	5 mins	10 mins

Servings:	Yield:
1	1 serving

Ingredients

- 8 baked scoop-shape tortilla chips
- 2 tablespoons refrigerated avocado dip (guacamole)
- ¼ cup chopped cherry tomatoes
- 1 tablespoon finely shredded reduced-fat cheddar cheese
- 1 tablespoon thinly sliced green onion

Directions

1. Place tortilla chips on a plate. Spoon avocado dip onto the chips. In a small bowl, combine cherry tomatoes, cheddar cheese, and green onion. Sprinkle mixture over chips.

https://www.eatingwell.com/recipe/263177/mini-nacho-cups/

Now that we've covered healthy habits, let's move on and develop accountability and take responsibility for your actions.

Step 6
Developing
Responsibility

Your actions are your responsibility, and taking responsibility for your actions is one of the greatest skills that one must have. Being responsible is a sign of maturity, and once you start being responsible and accountable for your actions, life will unravel better.

I used to forget to do my homework and miss deadlines, which stressed me. After that, I started making daily lists and setting reminders. It was difficult at first, but soon I felt a lot more organized. My teacher also praised me for turning in my homework on time. Being responsible makes me feel good and happy, and it is definitely worth it.

Some examples of being responsible are:

<u>Finishing school assignments on time</u>

<u>Keeping your room tidy</u>

<u>Admitting your mistakes</u>

<u>Being punctual</u>

<u>Respecting others</u>

Most of these things should come naturally to you. You should respect and treat others the way you want to be treated, and only by admitting your mistakes, will you be able to flourish and grow as a person.

When you admit your mistakes, your mind develops into accepting what is right and what is wrong. It is very important to trust yourself and be the best you can be, which is why every step taken should be taken very carefully because if anything goes wrong, you will be responsible for it.

If you trust yourself and can identify mistakes within yourself and work on them, no one can stop you from reaching all the potential you have stored inside you.

Things like keeping your room and surroundings tidy, keeping your dirty dishes in the sink after every meal, being punctual, etc., should be added to your everyday routine.

Along with this, you should also spend time with your family members. Spending time with people you love energizes your brain and relaxes you, increasing your productivity levels.

Responsibility applies to home as well as school. To be maintained in school, you should

- Submit your tasks on time
- Following school rules
- Punctuality, etc.

All the things mentioned are just some things that everyone should have but many people don't. Respect, self-love, responsibility, and kindness are some very basic things that people don't have. Being human means having emotions for yourself and the people around you. You need to be sensitive towards people and think before saying things as every person is different and it takes time to understand anyone and everyone.

Learning from your mistakes is the best way to learn something new in life. Life will create struggles for you so you can learn how to deal with them and until you deal with them, they will come back again and again until you fight and win. Learn from your mistakes because making mistakes isn't a weakness, it's a strength, an opportunity to become something better, something you weren't before, and every one of them will lead you to becoming a better person than you were.

Time for an **Activity**!!

Let's play Bingo. Cross out the tasks that you have done and aim to get a full house!

Complete a chore	Help a friend	Plan a project	Follow through on a commitment	Organize your space
Help with homework	Be on time	Set a goal	Take responsibility for a mistake	Clean up after yourself
Share something	Make a decision	Finish a task	Show respect to others	Manage your time well
Practice patience	Offer support	Complete a school assignment	Prepare for an event	Maintain a positive attitude
Help with family duties	Volunteer for a task	Organize your belongings	Stick to a schedule	Follow the rules and guidelines.

Step 7
Decision Making and Problem Solving

Coming to one of the most crucial steps towards self-management. Now that we all are growing up, it is very important to make important decisions on our own. These decisions can be small decisions like what food to eat or even deciding on choosing subjects for your career.

How to make good decisions?

First, it is very important to know what you want. It's very important to have a clear mind so that you can think about all the positive and negative consequences that come along with any decision you make.

How to make good decisions?

1. Know what you want. Figure out what you want and how will your choice support what you want.
2. Gather information: Learn more about the situation
3. Figure out all the possible consequences of that decision (Pros and Cons list!)
4. Act

Problem-solving?

There are 2 kinds of people on this Earth. One who finds problems, the other who finds solutions. We must become the second kind, which is why we need to understand how to seek solutions and have an answer for every problem.

How to find solutions?

The first step to finding a solution is to understand the problem. Ask yourself <u>'Can I do anything to fix this issue?'</u>, '<u>Who does it concern?</u>', '<u>What are the possible solutions to this problem</u>'.

The second you will start asking yourself 'why', 'what', and 'how', understanding the problem is going to become a lot easier.

Another important factor you need to consider while facing a problem is visualizing the after-effects. Imagine the solution you are thinking is done and put yourself in the scenario. How do you feel? Do you feel nice? Does it feel heavy on your chest? Do you feel guilty? The minute you start feeling emotions like sadness, guilt or even regret after visualizing this, you know that the solution you thought of isn't right.

EXAMPLE:

Problem: Sarah forgot her math homework at home and it's due today.

Solution: Sarah thinks about her options and makes a table to make it easier for her

Possible solutions	*Consequences*	*Close your eyes and imagine yourself after you have applied this solution. How do you feel?*

Make an excuse and lie about it.	I would feel like a liar. If my teacher finds out I will get into a lot of trouble and won't trust me again	I feel guilty, I feel like I shouldn't have lied
Tell the truth and submit pictures of it the minute I reach home	My teacher might scold me a bit, but she will believe me because I don't lie	I felt sad at first because I felt careless about leaving it at home but then it didn't bother me anymore because I did not lie so there was no guilt on my conscience.

She decides to tell her teacher what happened and asks if she can email a picture of the homework after school. The teacher agrees, and Sarah makes a reminder on her phone to send the homework as soon as she gets home.

Visualizing yourself after the task is done will allow your gut to respond which will make your decision clear.

EXAMPLE 2:

Problem: Jordan is deciding whether to apply for a summer internship at a local tech company or spend the summer preparing for an important school competition.

Solution: Jordan creates a detailed pros and cons list for each option.

Applying for the Internship:

PROS	CONS
Gain hands-on experience in the tech field	Limited time for personal study and relaxation
Build a professional network	May affect performance in the school competition if not managed well
Enhance his resume and college applications	
Learn practical skills and gain industry insight	

Preparing for the School Competition:

PROS	CONS
Focus on a specific goal and improve skills related to the competition	Miss out on valuable work experience and networking opportunities
Opportunity to potentially win and gain recognition	Limited exposure to real-world applications of skills
Less risk of disrupting his academic and personal balance	Might miss out on potential career opportunities in the tech field
No additional costs or commutes involved	No professional feedback or mentoring

Jordan understands how each option aligns with his long-term goals. The internship offers him a lot of career benefits but may come at the cost of personal time and his competition preparation. On the other hand, focusing on the competition could lead to achievements but then he would miss out on professional growth. As also visible, Jordan feels that the pros overpower the cons while considering applying for the internship, he decides to apply for the internship, planning to integrate preparation for the competition into his schedule to balance both opportunities.

Did you notice that Jordan matched his current decision to his long-term goals? This allowed him to plan for his future as well. This is also called 'foreseeing'. <u>Foresight</u> will allow you to think of every possible consequence of a decision, making you more prepared for the future.

Some ways you can foresee are: Talk to people who have experience or knowledge about the situation. They can provide valuable and different perspectives on the consequences that can take place.

: Think about what you will do if things don't go as planned. Have a backup plan to manage any negative consequences.

: Assess the likelihood and impact of each possible outcome. Balance potential risks against the benefits to determine the best choice.

EXAMPLE:

<u>Problem</u>: Taylor needs to decide whether to study abroad for a semester or stay at her current school and focus on her studies.

Solution: Taylor creates a detailed pros and cons list for each option.

Studying abroad:

PROS	CONS
Gain exposure to a new culture and learn a new language	Missing out on time with friends and family
Develop independence and adaptability	Potential challenges in keeping up with coursework and exams back home
Experience different academic and extracurricular activities	Adapting to a new environment and dealing with homesickness
Enhance her resume with international experience, which can be appealing to future employers or graduate programs	

Staying at Current School:

PROS	CONS
Continuity in studies with a familiar environment and support.	Lack of exposure to new cultures and global perspectives
Maintain friendships and stay close to family	Fewer opportunities for experiencing new challenges
Consistency in daily life and academic responsibilities	Missing out on a unique experience that could enhance personal and professional growth

Taylor looks at the pros and cons and decides that studying abroad would provide valuable experiences and growth opportunities, even though it involves higher costs and possible disruption to her academic routine. She prepares to face this challenge and make the most of her time abroad.

Moving ahead, sometimes you need to make decisions about people, relationships, etc. And for these decisions, you may not have time to make lists or charts. This is why there is a 3-step rule to make it easier to make fast decisions.

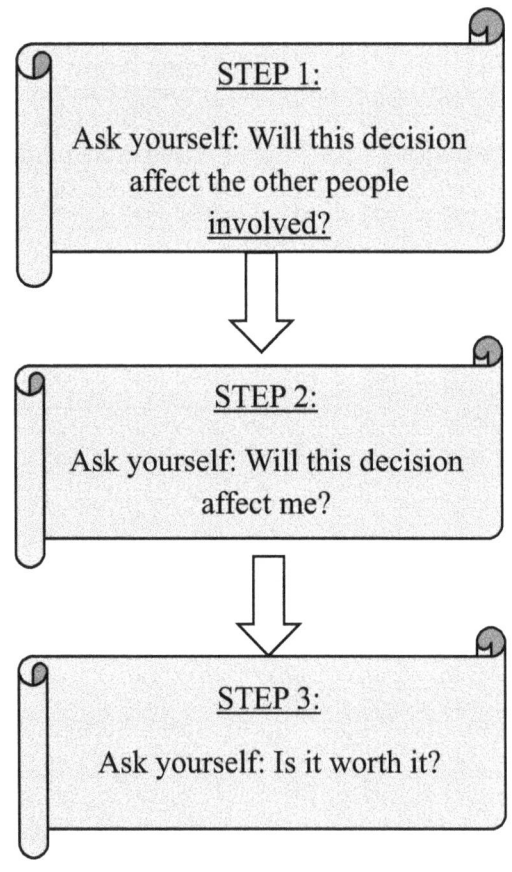

For example, I have fought with a friend of mine and I am planning on never talking to her again. Before taking this decision, I will ask myself 3 questions.

- "Will this decision affect the other people involved?" - The person involved in this case is my friend - and yes, it will affect her because we were very good friends and now, we don't talk.

- "Will this decision affect me?" - yes it will affect me because she is my very good friend, and I don't think I can lose her in a fight.

- "Is it worth it?" - In this case, breaking a friendship over a fight is not worth it.

These 3 steps would help me take this decision fast.

Make your own pros and cons list/consequence table/3 step method.

Problem:

Solution:

PROS	CONS

ACTIVITY 1:

DECISION MAKING SPIN THE WHEEL

Materials:

- A simple spinning wheel or spinner (you can make it using cardboard and colored paper)
- Decision-making scenarios written on the wheel segments

Prepare the Spinner: Create a spinner with different decision-making scenarios for each segment. Examples:

- "Choose between going to a movie or visiting a friend."
- "Decide whether to save or spend ₹10."

Spin and Decide: Players take turns spinning the wheel. When the spinner stops, they read the scenario and make a decision.

Discuss: Briefly discuss the decision and its possible outcomes.

Step 8
Staying Motivated

At times, we feel lazy and don't want to do much. How do we motivate ourselves? How do we tell ourselves that we can do it, and we can do it now?

The first step is <u>celebrating</u>. Celebrate yourself and your victories every day. Congratulate yourself for doing everything you can. Treat yourself to a bar of chocolate if you clean your room. Watch your favorite movie if you finish all your work on time. Celebrate your effort and feel proud of yourself. Celebrating your small wins is the first step to motivating yourself.

Have a resilient mindset. Resilience is the ability to bounce back from setbacks and adapt to challenges smoothly and easily. It's essential for handling and tackling life's ups and downs smoothly and easily.

Setbacks like academic challenges, sports injuries, not being able to achieve personal goals, or even social conflicts, can bring you down, destroying your mood. What to do in such cases?

Stay positive. Reset your goals by making them easier and more achievable, seek help from more experienced people, and most importantly learn from your setbacks. You encounter a setback when you make a mistake. Learn from your mistakes so the next time you are in a similar situation, you know your way out.

Be positive in all situations because it is the positivity that gives u the glimmer of hope that carries you forward.

Always have a growth mindset. A growth mindset is the belief that talents and skills can be developed through dedication, hard work, and education. People with a growth mindset view challenges as opportunities to grow and see failure as a steppingstone to improvement.

utilizing a growth mindset can increase your ability to learn. It allows you to bounce back from a setback and adapt more easily to a new situation. Using this strategy encourages a positive attitude toward learning and personal growth, making it easier to overcome obstacles and achieve your goals.

Difference between a fixed and a growth mindset:

FIXED MINDSET

- Example: Jamie finds math challenging and thinks, "I'm just not good at math." Jamie avoids math problems and doesn't seek help, believing that their abilities are static and unchangeable.
- Belief: "My abilities are fixed, and I can't change them."

GROWTH MINDSET

- Example: Alex struggles with math but believes that with practice and effort, he can improve. He seeks help, studies hard, and gradually improves his skills in his desired criteria.
- Belief: "I can learn and grow through effort and practice because practice makes perfect."

Another term we will be talking about is 'Perseverance'

Perseverance is the ability to continue working toward a goal despite obstacles or delays. It is crucial because it:

1. **Achieves Goals**: Helps individuals push through obstacles and stay focused on their long-term objectives.

2. **Builds Confidence**: Strengthens self-belief by demonstrating that persistence can lead to success.

3. **Fosters Growth**: Encourages learning and development by overcoming challenges and setbacks.

4. **Enhances Problem-Solving**: Develops critical thinking and problem-solving skills through continuous effort.

Examples:

- Naina struggled in Math but continued practicing every day, seeking help, and was more attentive. Gradually, she improved her grades and excelled in the subject.

- Jordan got several injuries while training for a marathon but kept working hard and practicing despite his wound. His perseverance led him to complete the marathon successfully.

- Alex aimed to learn a new language. Despite initial difficulties and slow progress, he continued practicing and eventually became fluent.

Tips for Developing Resilience and Perseverance

1. **Set Clear Goals**: Define what you want to achieve and create a plan with actionable steps. This will help you be motivated and will help you keep on moving forward

2. **Stay Positive**: Keep a positive mindset, even when facing constant setbacks. Believe in yourself and your ability to overcome challenges.

3. **Embrace Challenges**: View your obstacles as opportunities to grow, experience, and learn. Accept that difficulties are part of the journey which will only help you become better.

4. **Seek Support**: Talk and connect with friends, family, or mentors for encouragement and advice when facing tough times.

5. **Practice Self-Care**: Maintain physical and mental health through regular exercise, healthy eating, and relaxation techniques to stay strong and motivated.

6. **Reflect and Adapt**: Regularly review your progress, learn from setbacks, and adjust your strategies as needed to keep moving forward.

Sometimes, when we put our time into something and it doesn't come out as expected to be, we go into this phase of disappointment. Instead of feeling disappointed and lost, be proud that you worked hard. Celebrate the effort you gave. If you had never given the effort, you would have never known the value of trying. Even if the effort you gave did not reach you where you wanted to be, now you know that you need to make more effort. Plus, it's not like the effort given was pointless because, throughout that journey, you were constantly learning something, and even if it didn't help you reach where you wanted to be, you grew as a person, learned from your mistakes, and kept moving on, which is the real part of being proud about. And always remember, effort is visible so whatever effort you give to anyone or anything, it's never in vain.

ACTIVITY!

Materials Needed:

- A blank notebook or journal

- Colored pens, markers, or stickers

1. Decorate Your Journal: Start by decorating the cover of your journal with stickers, drawings, or designs that represent your interests and personality. Make it your very own "Adventure Journal"!

2. Daily Prompts: Each day or week, use one of the following prompts given below to reflect on your experiences.

3. Adventure Challenges: After understanding and answering each prompt, set an easy and small "growth

challenge" for yourself. This could be trying a new activity, practicing a skill, or tackling something that feels difficult.

4. Celebrate Progress: At the end of each week, review your entries and challenges. Celebrate your progress with a sticker or a fun drawing that represents your achievements.

Journal Prompts: -

1. Challenge Accepted: "What was a recent challenge I faced? How did I tackle it, and what did I learn from the experience?"

2. Growth Goals: "What is something new I want to learn or improve? What steps will I take to achieve this goal?"

3. Oops, I Failed!: "Describe a time when something didn't go as planned. How did I respond, and what did I learn from this experience?"

4. Celebration Time: "What is one accomplishment I'm proud of this week? How did my effort and persistence contribute to this success?"

5. Support Squad: "Who helped me overcome a challenge, and how did their support make a difference? How can I be a good friend and support others?"

You can also add these:

- My Challenge Story: (a recent challenge and lessons learned)

- Growth Goal Setting: (describe a new skill or goal and the steps to achieve it)

- Learning from Mistakes: (write about a mistake and what was learned)

- Celebrate My Success: (describe an accomplishment and the effort involved)

- My Support Squad: (write about someone who helped and how it made a difference)

Activity 2: Make a poster!

Take an A3 size sheet, decorate it however you want it, and write a few growth mindsets and motivational affirmative quotes on it

Quotes you can use:

- *"The only limit to our realization of tomorrow is our doubts of today."* – Franklin D. Roosevelt

- *"The more that you read, the more things you will know. The more that you learn, the more places you'll go."* – Dr. Seuss

- *"Success is not final, failure is not fatal: It is the courage to continue that counts."* – Winston Churchill

- *"Your mind is a garden. Your thoughts are the seeds. You can grow flowers, or you can grow weeds."* - Dr. Seuss

- *"Believe you can and you're halfway there."* – Theodore Roosevelt

- *"Mistakes are proof that you are trying."* – Jennifer Lim

- *"The only way to achieve the impossible is to believe it is possible."* – Charles Kingsleigh (Alice in Wonderland)

- *"You have brains in your head. You have feet in your shoes. You can steer yourself in any direction you choose."* – Dr. Seuss.

- *"You miss 100% of the shots you don't take."* – Wayne Gretzky

- *"It always seems impossible until it's done."* – Nelson Mandela

- *"Don't measure your value with someone else's tape"* – Les Brown

Here, you end the journey of learning about yourself and managing things. Time to reflect!

Reflecting on past experiences is an important part of personal development and self-management. It helps us understand our strengths and areas for improvement, helping us make better decisions in the future.

Everything we do, everything we learn, changes our path. We think about our education to understand and enjoy it. This is important because it helps you grow, learn new skills and achieve your goals. By constantly looking for ways to improve, you can be successful and confident in everything you do!

Use this format to have a rough layout for your goals so you are on track:

Goal 1:

- What I Want to Achieve:
  _____

- Steps to Achieve This Goal:
  _____

- Timeline: _____
- Progress Tracking:
  _____

Goal 2:

- What I Want to Achieve:
  _____

- Steps to Achieve This Goal:
  _____

- Timeline: _____

- Progress Tracking:
  _____

Goal 3:

- What I Want to Achieve:
  _____

- Steps to Achieve This Goal:
  _____

- Timeline: _____

- Progress Tracking:
  _____

To finish this journey, rate yourself out of 10 for each category:

Category	Rating (out of 10)
Time Management and Prioritization	
Organizational Skills	
Goal Setting and Achievement	

Self-Discipline and Focus	
Stress Management Techniques	
Problem-Solving Abilities	
Adaptability to Change	
Responsibility for Actions	
Decision-Making Skills	
Reflective Practice and Improvement	

Now compare yourself to what you were when you hadn't read this book. Do you see a difference? If not, keep on practicing, you will get there!

Always remember, *our strengths define us. Our weaknesses turned into strengths redefine us.*

www.ingramcontent.com/pod-product-compliance
Lightning Source LLC
LaVergne TN
LVHW061625070526
838199LV00070B/6587